Piano

John Kember

# Piano Sight-Reading 2

## Déchiffrage pour le piano 2
## Vom-Blatt-Spiel auf dem Klavier 2

*A fresh approach / Nouvelle approche*
*Eine erfrischend neue Methode*

ED 12791
ISMN M-2201-2316-0

www.schott-music.com

Mainz · London · Madrid · New York · Paris · Prague · Tokyo · Toronto

**Acknowledgements**
We wish to thank: Blackheath Conservatoire of Music, London, Gareth Bucket, John Caudwell, Tom Dodd, Andrew Haigh, John and Nathan Hayward, Simon Proctor, David Sams and Claire Williams for their valued support, advice and encouragement in the preparation of this book.

**Remerciements**
Nous tenons à remercier le Conservatoire de musique de Blackheath (Londres), Gareth Bucket, John Caudwell, Tom Dodd, Andrew Haigh, John et Nathan Hayward, Simon Proctor, David Sams et Claire Williams de leur soutien, de leurs conseils et de leurs encouragements inestimables lors de la préparation de ce recueil.

**Danksagung**
Wir möchten uns bei dem Blackheath Conservatoire of Music London, Gareth Bucket, John Caudwell, Tom Dodd, Andrew Haigh, John und Nathan Hayward, Simon Proctor, David Sams und Claire Williams für ihre wertvolle Unterstützung, ihren Rat und ihre Bestärkung bei der Herstellung dieses Buches bedanken.

ED 12791

British Library Cataloguing-in-Publication Data.
A catalogue record for this book is available from the British Library.
ISMN M-2201-2316-0
ISBN 1-902455-23-1



French translation: Agnès Ausseur
German translation: Esther Dubielzig
Design by www.adamhaystudio.com
Music setting by Willems Notensatz, Villingen-Schwenningen
Printed in Germany S&Co.7978

# Contents

## Sommaire/Inhalt

# Preface

*Piano Sight-Reading 2* builds on the progress achieved by following the outlines and good practice established in Book 1.

Ideally, sight-reading in some form should be a regular part of a student's routine each time they go to a piano, and it is of even greater value if their efforts are heard – in part or entirely – by a teacher at the following lesson.

This book helps to establish the habit of regular sight-reading, generally recognised as a vital skill in all fields of music. To this end, the exercises are progressive and structured to increase the pupil's awareness of new rhythms, keys and range of notes. Changes of hand position are introduced gradually, as is the recognition of and familiarity with chord shapes in both 2- and 3-note groups. The initial exercises however make no changes of hand position, but remain the same throughout.

Finally, both hands are treated equally, with all exercises requiring hands together.

## To the pupil: Why sight-reading?

When faced with a new piece at home, in a lesson, in a rehearsal, playing with other instrumentalists, or in an audition or examination, there is no one there to help you. *You are on your own!*

Regular sight-reading practice enables you gradually to build your knowledge and experience, and above all, your confidence to be able to make a successful attempt.

This is a book for the student rather than the teacher. It takes you stage by stage, beginning with simple 'hands together' pieces with no position changes through gaining familiarity with semiquavers in 2/4 and 3/8 times, making position changes in each hand before making changes in both hands together, introduces 2- then 3-note chord shapes, and finally new keys up to two sharps and flats.

*Try to read something new – however short – each time you sit at the piano.*

Becoming a good sight-reader is one of the most, if not the most, important skill you can acquire as an instrumentalist and musician.

Remember, always consider a new piece simply as a rhythm first. Tap, clap or even sing it, and you will get a feeling for the style and shape before you play a note.

Think of these as 'mini-pieces' and try to learn each one quickly and correctly, then when you are faced with real sight-reading you will be well equipped to succeed on a first attempt.

# Préface

*Déchiffrage pour le piano 2* s'appuie sur les progrès faits grâce à la méthode et aux bonnes habitudes acquises par le travail du premier recueil.

L'idéal serait que le déchiffrage, sous quelque forme que ce soit, prenne régulièrement place dans la routine de travail de l'élève à chaque fois qu'il se met au piano. Cette démarche acquerra encore plus de valeur si son travail est entendu - en partie ou entièrement - par son professeur à la leçon suivante.

Ce recueil facilitera l'habitude régulière du déchiffrage, dont la capacité est unanimement considérée comme essentielle dans tous les domaines de la musique. Dans cet objectif, les exercices sont progressifs et structurés de manière à augmenter l'ouverture à de nouveaux rythmes, tonalité et étendues de notes. Les changements de position des mains sont introduits progressivement ainsi que les notions d'accords, sous forme d'intervalles ou d'accords de trois sons, et la familiarisation à leur usage. Les premiers exercices, toutefois, ne présentent pas de changements de position de la main qui reste stable d'un bout à l'autre.

Enfin, les deux mains sont traitées à égalité, tous les exercices devant être exécutés mains ensemble.

## A l'élève : Pourquoi le déchiffrage ?

Lorsque vous vous trouvez face à un nouveau morceau, que ce soit chez vous, pendant une leçon, lors d'une répétition, en jouant avec d'autres instrumentistes ou pendant une audition ou un examen, personne d'autre que vous-même ne peut vous aider. Vous êtes seul !

La pratique régulière du déchiffrage vous permettra peu à peu d'affermir vos connaissances, votre expérience et, surtout, votre confiance en votre capacité à réussir dès la première lecture. Ce recueil s'adresse plus à l'élève qu'au professeur. Il vous guidera, étape par étape, en commençant par des pièces mains ensemble simples, sans changements de position, vers l'entraînement aux mouvements de doubles croches dans des mesures à 2/4 et à 3/8, les changements de position à chaque main, puis aux deux mains, l'initiation aux formules d'accords sous forme d'intervalles puis d'accords de trois sons et, enfin, vers de nouvelles tonalités comprenant jusqu'à deux dièses et deux bémols.

*Efforcez-vous de retenir un élément nouveau, même très court, chaque fois que vous vous asseyez au piano.*

Devenir un bon déchiffreur est l'une des capacités les plus importantes, sinon la plus importante, que vous puissiez acquérir en tant qu'instrumentiste et musicien.

N'oubliez pas de toujours envisager un nouveau morceau d'abord comme un rythme. Battez-le, frappez-le dans les mains, chantez-le même, vous en reconnaîtrez le style et la forme avant d'en avoir joué une note.

Considérez ces exercices comme des « mini-morceaux » et essayez de les apprendre rapidement et sans erreur, ainsi, face à un véritable déchiffrage, vous serez bien équipé pour réussir dès la première lecture.

# Vorwort

*Vom-Blatt-Spiel auf dem Klavier 2* behält das in Band 1 eingeführte Konzept und die Übetechnik bei und baut auf den bisher gemachten Fortschritten auf.

Im Idealfall sollte das Vom-Blatt-Spiel in irgendeiner Form zu einem festen Bestandteil im Übeprogramm des Schülers werden, wann immer er sich an das Klavier setzt.
Noch sinnvoller ist es, wenn das Ergebnis in der darauffolgenden Unterrichtsstunde vom Lehrer ganz oder teilweise überprüft wird.

Ziel dieser Ausgabe ist es, den Schüler dazu zu bringen, sich regelmäßiges Vom-Blatt-Spiel anzugewöhnen, was überall in der Musik als unerlässlich angesehen wird.
Zu diesem Zweck sind die Übungen progressiv angelegt und darauf ausgerichtet, das Gefühl des Schülers für neue Rhythmen, Tonarten und Notenräume zu verbessern.
Nach und nach werden verschiedene Handpositionen sowie das Erkennen von und der vertraute Umgang mit Zweiton- und Dreitonakkorden eingeführt. Die Anfangsübungen erfordern allerdings keine Positionswechsel der Hand, sondern behalten die Handposition durchgehend bei.

Beide Hände werden gleich behandelt; dabei erfordern alle Übungen den gleichzeitigen Einsatz beider Hände.

## An den Schüler: Warum Vom-Blatt-Spiel?

Wenn du zuhause, im Unterricht, bei einer Probe, beim Spiel mit anderen Instrumentalisten, bei einem Vorspiel oder bei einer Prüfung mit einem neuen Stück konfrontiert wirst, gibt es niemanden, der dir dabei helfen kann.
*Du bist auf dich allein gestellt!*

Durch regelmäßiges Üben des Vom-Blatt-Spiels wirst du allmählich deine Kenntnisse und Erfahrungen ausweiten – und vor allem dein Selbstvertrauen in die eigenen Fähigkeiten stärken.

Dieser Band richtet sich vornehmlich an den Schüler als an den Lehrer. Die Lernschwerpunkte werden abschnittweise eingeführt: beginnend mit einfachen Stücken zum Zweihändigspielen ohne Positionswechsel, über den verstärkten Umgang mit Sechzehnteln im 2/4- und 3/8-Takt, Positionswechsel in jeder einzelnen Hand, bevor Positionswechsel in beiden Händen gleichzeitig stattfinden, bis hin zur Einführung von Zweiton- und Dreitonakkorden und neuen Tonarten mit bis zu zwei Kreuz- und ♭-Vorzeichen.

*Versuche jedes Mal, wenn du dich ans Klavier setzt, etwas Neues vom Blatt zu spielen, wie kurz es auch sein mag.*

Gut vom Blatt spielen zu können ist eine der wichtigsten, wenn nicht die wichtigste Fähigkeit, die man als Instrumentalist und Musiker erwerben kann.

Denk daran, bei jedem neuen Stück ist zunächst immer nur der Rhythmus wichtig. Klopfe, klatsche oder singe ihn! Dann wirst du ein Gefühl für Stil und Form bekommen, bevor du überhaupt eine einzige Note gespielt hast.

Behandle die folgenden Übungen als „Mini-Stücke“ und versuche, jede schnell und fehlerlos zu erlernen. Wenn du dann tatsächlich einmal vom Blatt spielen musst, wirst du gut gerüstet sein und gleich beim ersten Versuch Erfolg haben.

# Part 1

## 1ère Partie / Teil 1

**Remember:**

**Always** look at the *time signature* first.
**Always** clap, tap or sing the *rhythm.*
**Always** check the *key signature.*
Where are the *sharps* and *flats?*
**Always** be aware of the *key* you are playing in.
**Always** find the *correct position* for each hand to begin.
**Always** try to *watch the music* and not your hands!

**Rappels:**

**Toujours** regarder l'indication de *mesure* d'abord.
**Toujours** battre le *rythme* ou le frapper dans les mains ou le chanter.
**Toujours** vérifier *l'armure* de la clef, quels sont les *dièses* ou les *bémol.*
**Toujours** garder à l'esprit la *tonalité* dans laquelle on joue
**Toujours** rechercher la *position correcte* de chaque main pour commencer
**Toujours** s'efforcer de *lire la musique* et de ne pas regarder les mains.

**Denk daran:**

**Immer** zuerst nach der *Taktvorzeichnung* sehen.
**Immer** den *Rhythmus* klatschen, klopfen oder singen.
**Immer** die *Tonartvorzeichnung* beachten. Wo stehen *Kreuze* und ♭'s?
**Immer** die *Tonart* merken, in der man spielt.
**Immer** für jede Hand die *richtige Position* herausfinden, mit der man anfängt.
**Immer** versuchen, auf die *Noten zu sehen* und nicht auf die eigenen Hände!

# 1. Simple hands together
# 1. Lecture mains ensemble simple
# *1. Beide Hände gleichzeitig zusammen*

Both hands remain in the same position throughout.

**Remember:**
**Always** look at the *time signature* first.
**Always** clap, tap or sing the *rhythm.*
**Always** check the *key signature.* Where are the *sharps* and *flats?*
**Always** be aware of the *key* you are playing in.
**Always** find the *correct position* for each hand to begin.
**Always** try to *watch the music* and not your hands!

Les deux mains gardent la même position d'un bout à l'autre.

**Rappels:**
**Toujours** regarder l'indication de *mesure* d'abord.
**Toujours** battre le *rythme* ou le frapper dans les mains ou le chanter.
**Toujours** vérifier *l'armure* de la clef, quels sont les *dièses* ou les *bémol.*
**Toujours** garder à l'esprit de *tonalité* dans laquelle on joue.
**Toujours** rechercher la *position correcte* de chaque main pour commencer.
**Toujours** s'efforcer de *lire la musique* et de ne pas regarder les mains!

Beide Hände bleiben durchgehend in derselben Position.

**Denk daran:**
**Immer** zuerst nach der *Taktvorzeichnung* sehen.
**Immer** den *Rhythmus* klatschen, klopfen oder singen.
**Immer** die *Tonartvorzeichnung* beachten. Wo stehen *Kreuze* und *♭'s?*
**Immer** die *Tonart* merken, in der man spielt.
**Immer** für jede Hand die *richtige Position* herausfinden, mit der man anfängt.
**Immer** versuchen, auf die *Noten zu sehen* und nicht auf die eigene Hände!

1. **Moderato**

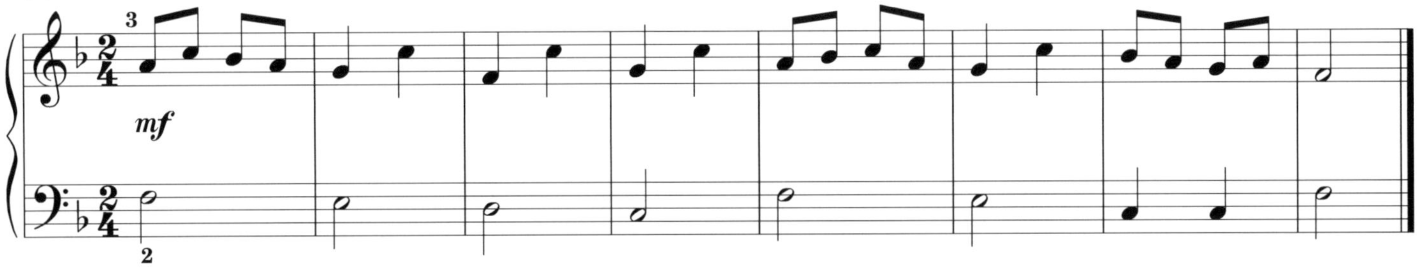

3

*mf*

2

2. **Leisurely**

5

*mf*

3

5

3. **Andante**

5
mf
4. In slow Waltz time
4
mf
p
2
marcato
5
5. In Waltz tempo
1
mp
1
5
6. In March time
3
mf
5
5

## 7. Moderato

It will always help to count a full bar before you begin.

Il sera toujours utile de compter une mesure complète avant de commencer.

Es hilft immer, einen ganzen Takt zu zählen, bevor man zu spielen anfängt.

## 8. Legato

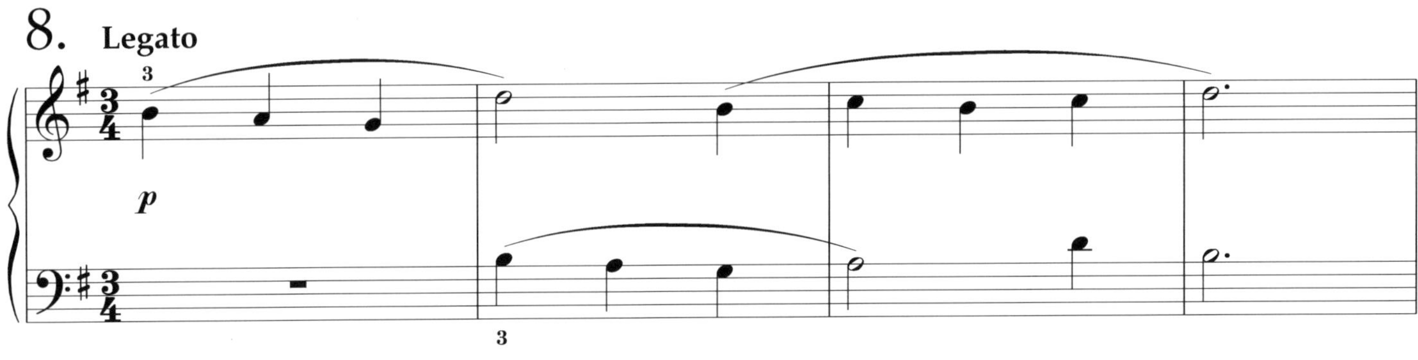

Do you know which key you are in? The last and lowest note is usually a reliable guide.

Savez-vous dans quelle tonalité vous êtes? La dernière note la plus grave est généralement une indication fiable.

Weißt du, in welcher Tonart du dich befindest? Die letzte und niedrigste Note ist in der Regel ein guter Anhaltspunkt.

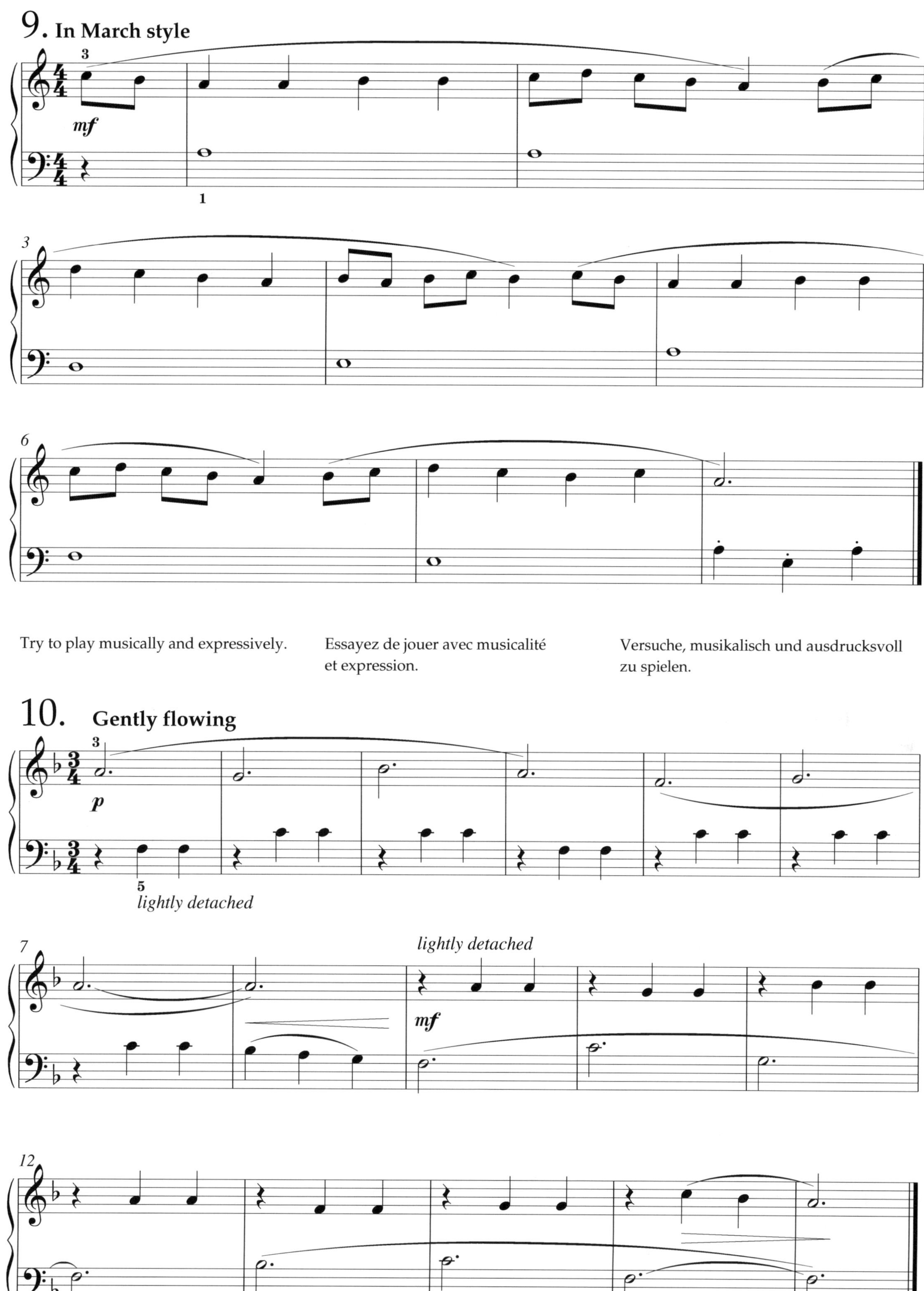
9. In March style
3
mf
1
3
6
Try to play musically and expressively.
Essayez de jouer avec musicalité et expression.
Versuche, musikalisch und ausdrucksvoll zu spielen.
10. Gently flowing
3
p
5
lightly detached
7
lightly detached
mf
12

## 11. With movement

Try to play musically and expressively.

Essayez de jouer avec musicalité et expression.

Versuche, musikalisch und ausdrucksvoll zu spielen.

## 12. Cantabile

It will always help to count a full bar before you begin.

Il sera toujours utile de compter une mesure complète avant de commencer.

Es hilft immer, einen ganzen Takt zu zählen, bevor man zu spielen anfängt.

## 13. In March style

14. Dolce
mp
15. Sadly
p
16. Gently flowing
mp

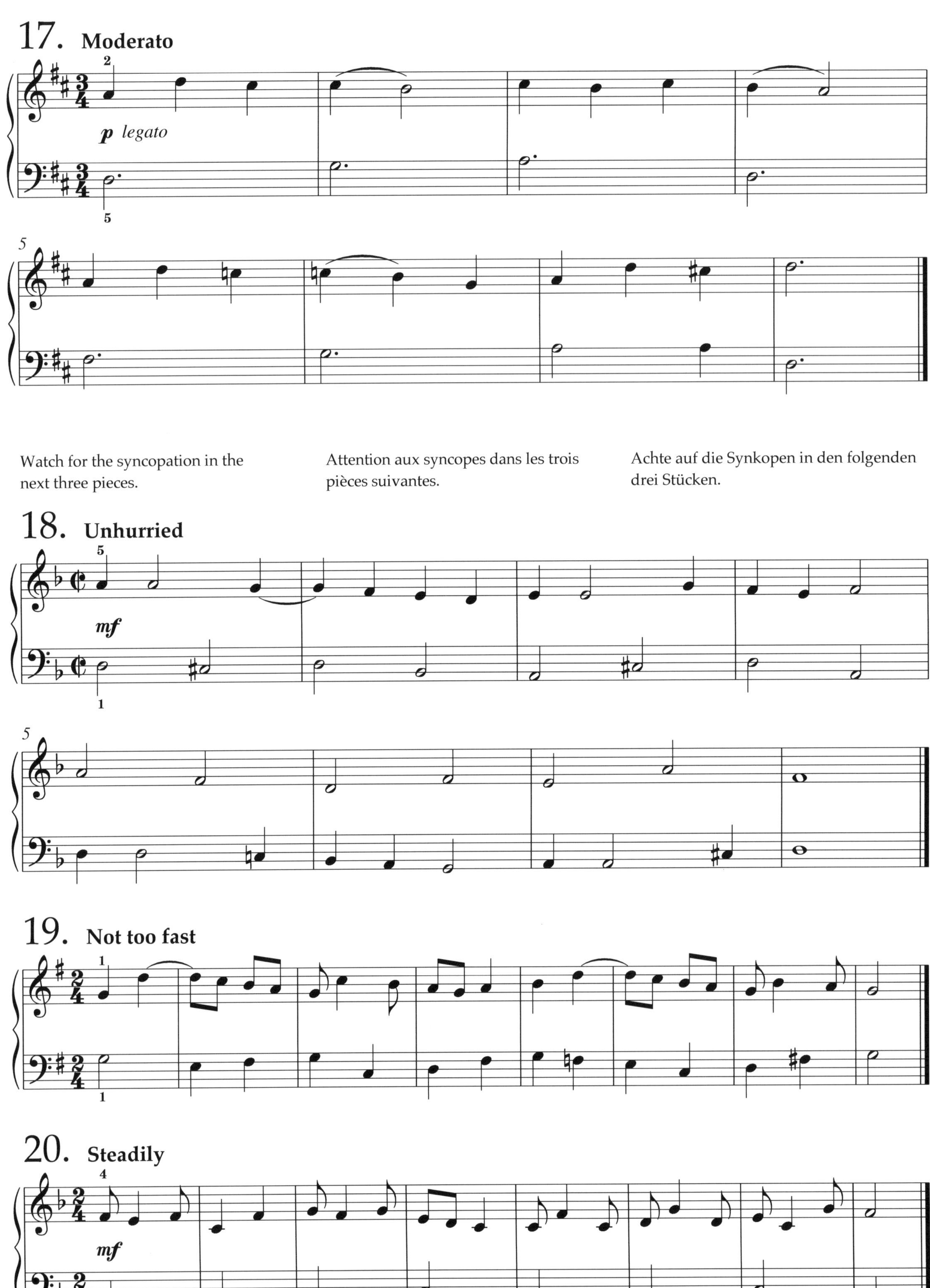


Watch for the syncopation in the next three pieces.

Attention aux syncopes dans les trois pièces suivantes.

Achte auf die Synkopen in den folgenden drei Stücken.

## 2. Semiquavers in 2/4-time
## 2. Doubles croches dans une mesure à 2/4
## *2. Sechzehntel im 2/4-Takt*

It helps to count the half beats (quavers) when playing semiquavers.

**Remember:**
**Always** look at the *time signature* first.
**Always** clap, tap or sing the *rhythm.*
**Always** check the *key signature.* Where are the *sharps* and *flats?*
**Always** be aware of the *key* you are playing in.
**Always** find the *correct position* for each hand to begin.
**Always** try to *watch the music* and not your hands!

Compter les demis temps (croches) facilite l'exécution des doubles croches.

**Rappels:**
**Toujours** regarder l'indication de *mesure* d'abord.
**Toujours** battre le *rythme* ou le frapper dans les mains ou le chanter.
**Toujours** vérifier *l'armure* de la clef, quels sont les *dièses* ou les *bémol.*
**Toujours** garder à l'esprit de *tonalité* dans laquelle on joue.
**Toujours** rechercher la *position correcte* de chaque main pour commencer.
**Toujours** s'efforcer de *lire la musique* et de ne pas regarder les mains!

Es hilft, beim Spielen von Sechzehntelnoten die halben Schläge (Achtel) zu zählen.

**Denk daran:**
**Immer** zuerst nach der *Taktvorzeichnung* sehen.
**Immer** den *Rhythmus* klatschen, klopfen oder singen.
**Immer** die *Tonartvorzeichnung* beachten. Wo stehen *Kreuze* und ♭'*s?*
**Immer** die *Tonart* merken, in der man spielt.
**Immer** für jede Hand die *richtige Position* herausfinden, mit der man anfängt.
**Immer** versuchen, auf die *Noten zu sehen* und nicht auf die eigene Hände!

Remember, always clap, tap or sing the rhythm first.

N'oubliez pas de toujours d'abord battre, frapper dans les mains ou chanter le rythme.

Denk daran – immer zuerst den Rhythmus klatschen, klopfen oder singen.

## 26. Not too fast

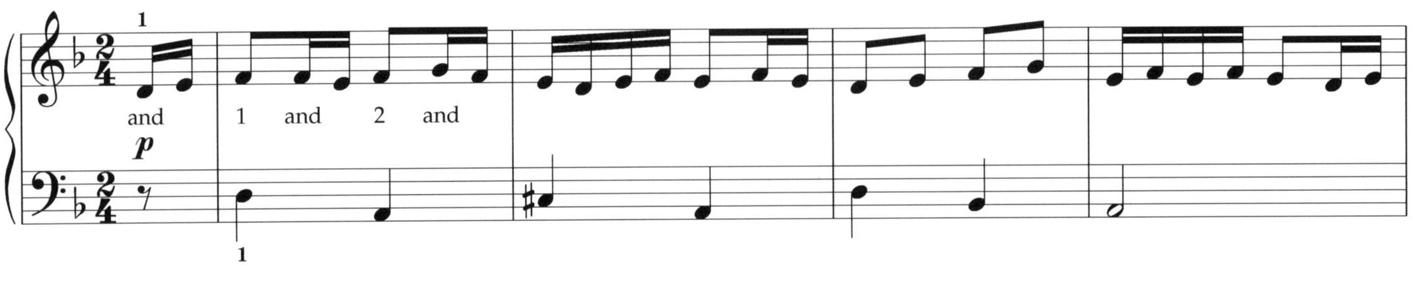

If your piece begins on any beat of the bar other than the first, count yourself in.

Si la pièce commence sur un autre temps que le premier, comptez la mesure entière.

Wenn dein Stück auf einem anderen als dem ersten Schlag des Taktes beginnt, zähle den Takt an.

## 28. Ragtime

5

*mf*

5

5

## 29. In the style of a Gavotte

3

*p leggiero*

2

4

# 3. Semiquavers in 3/8 time
# 3. Doubles croches dans une mesure à 3/8
# *3. Sechzehntel im 3/8-Takt*

**Remember:**
**Always** look at the *time signature* first.
**Always** clap, tap or sing the *rhythm.*
**Always** check the *key signature.*
Where are the *sharps* and *flats?*
**Always** be aware of the *key* you are playing in.
**Always** find the *correct position* for each hand to begin.
**Always** try to *watch the music* and not your hands!

**Rappels:**
**Toujours** regarder l'indication de *mesure* d'abord.
**Toujours** battre le *rythme* ou le frapper dans les mains ou le chanter.
**Toujours** vérifier *l'armure* de la clef, quels sont les *dièses* ou les *bémol.*
**Toujours** garder à l'esprit de *tonalité* dans laquelle on joue.
**Toujours** rechercher la *position correcte* de chaque main pour commencer.
**Toujours** s'efforcer de *lire la musique* et de ne pas regarder les mains!

**Denk daran:**
**Immer** zuerst nach der *Taktvorzeichnung* sehen.
**Immer** den *Rhythmus* klatschen, klopfen oder singen.
**Immer** die *Tonartvorzeichnung* beachten. Wo stehen *Kreuze* und ♭'s?
**Immer** die *Tonart* merken, in der man spielt.
**Immer** für jede Hand die *richtige Position* herausfinden, mit der man anfängt.
**Immer** versuchen, auf die *Noten zu sehen* und nicht auf die eigene Hände!

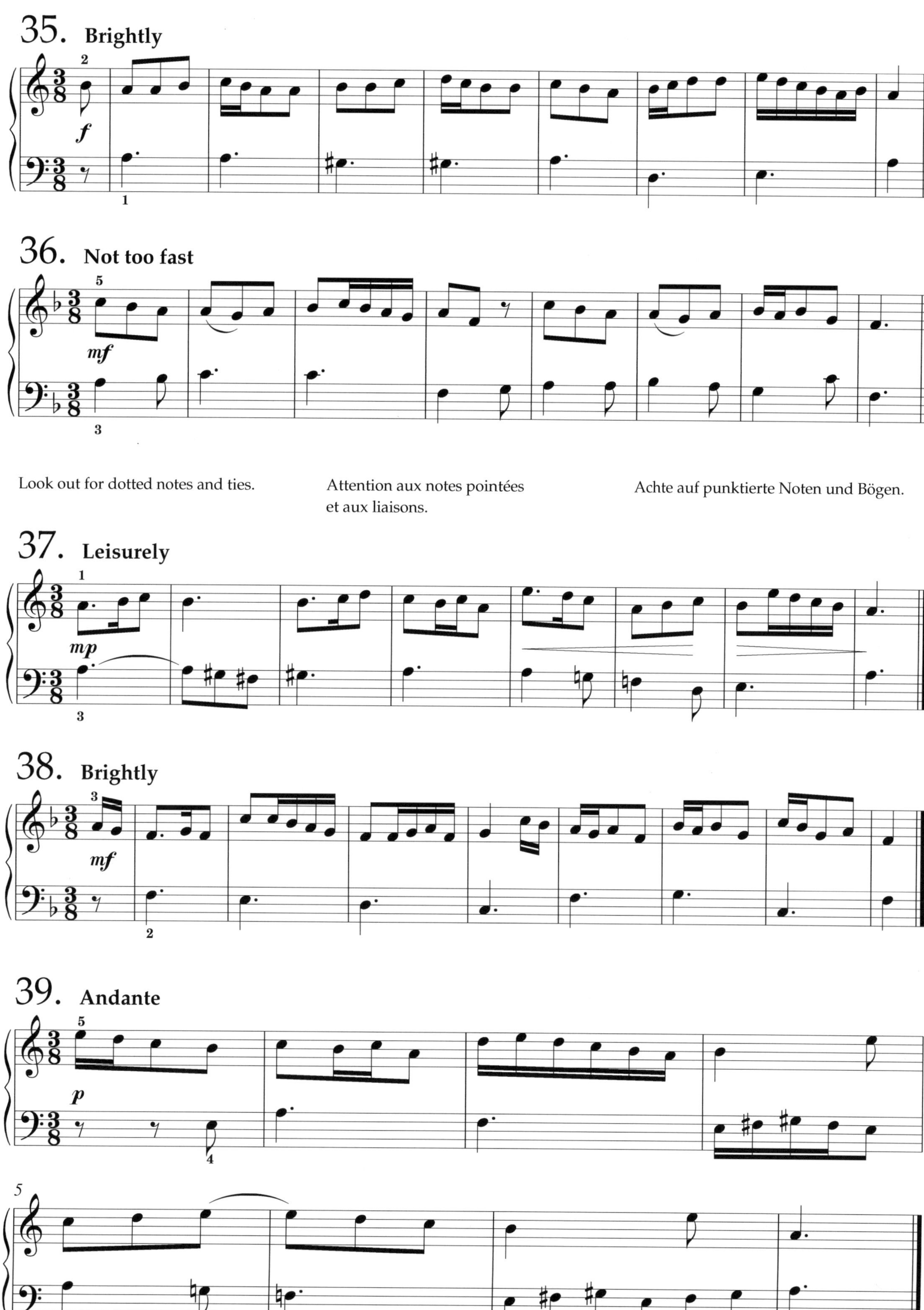
35. Brightly
f
36. Not too fast
mf
Look out for dotted notes and ties.
Attention aux notes pointées et aux liaisons.
Achte auf punktierte Noten und Bögen.
37. Leisurely
mp
38. Brightly
mf
39. Andante
p

# 4. Position changes in the right hand
# 4. Changement de position de la main droite
# *4. Positionswechsel in der rechten Hand*

Numbers above the right-hand stave indicate a change of position.

Les chiffres placés au-dessus de la portée indiquent les changements de position.

Die Ziffern über dem Liniensystem der rechten Hand zeigen einen Positionswechsel an.

**Remember:**
**Always** look at the *time signature* first.
**Always** clap, tap or sing the *rhythm.*
**Always** check the *key signature.* Where are the *sharps* and *flats?*
**Always** be aware of the *key* you are playing in.
**Always** find the *correct position* for each hand to begin.
**Always** try to *watch the music* and not your hands!

**Rappels:**
**Toujours** regarder l'indication de *mesure* d'abord.
**Toujours** battre le *rythme* ou le frapper dans les mains ou le chanter.
**Toujours** vérifier *l'armure* de la clef, quels sont les *dièses* ou les *bémol.*
**Toujours** garder à l'esprit de *tonalité* dans laquelle on joue.
**Toujours** rechercher la *position correcte* de chaque main pour commencer.
**Toujours** s'efforcer de *lire la musique* et de ne pas regarder les mains!

**Denk daran:**
**Immer** zuerst nach der *Taktvorzeichnung* sehen.
**Immer** den *Rhythmus* klatschen, klopfen oder singen.
**Immer** die *Tonartvorzeichnung* beachten. Wo stehen *Kreuze* und ♭'s?
**Immer** die *Tonart* merken, in der man spielt.
**Immer** für jede Hand die *richtige Position* herausfinden, mit der man anfängt.
**Immer** versuchen, auf die *Noten zu sehen* und nicht auf die eigene Hände!

## 40. In March style

## 41. Gently flowing

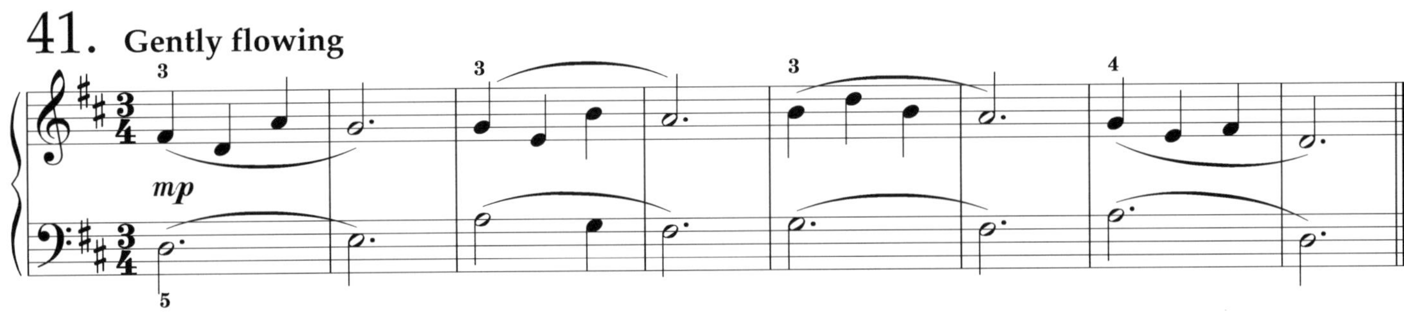


## 42. Moderato

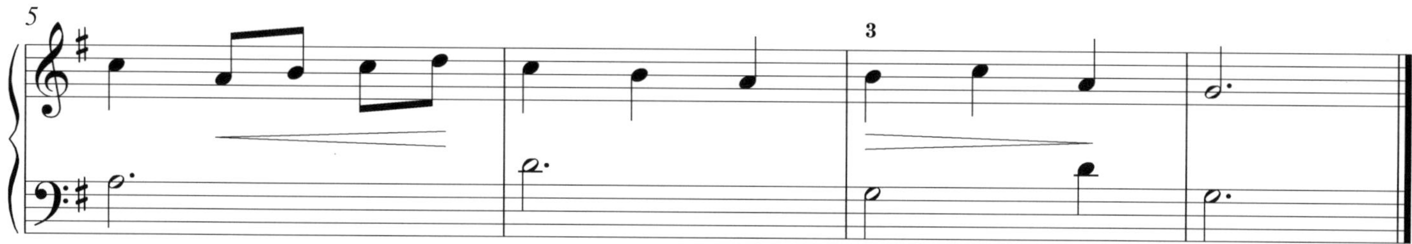

Set yourself a realistic tempo. Always look at the tempo/style indication given.

Prenez un tempo raisonnable. Regardez toujours les indications de tempo et de style données.

Wähle ein realistisches Tempo. Achte immer auf die notierten Tempo/Stilangaben.

## 43. Steadily

## 44. Flowing

## 45. Vivace

## 46. Not too fast

Do you know which key you are in? The last and lowest note is usually a reliable guide.

Savez-vous dans quelle tonalité vous êtes? La dernière note la plus grave est généralement une indication fiable.

Weißt du, in welcher Tonart du dich befindest? Die letzte und niedrigste Note ist in der Regel ein guter Anhaltspunkt.

## 47. Andante

## 48. Andante

## 49. Lively

If your piece begins on any beat of the bar other than the first, count yourself in.

Si la pièce commence sur un autre temps que le premier, comptez la mesure entière.

Wenn dein Stück auf einem anderen als dem ersten Schlag des Taktes beginnt, zähle den Takt an.

## 50. Quite slowly

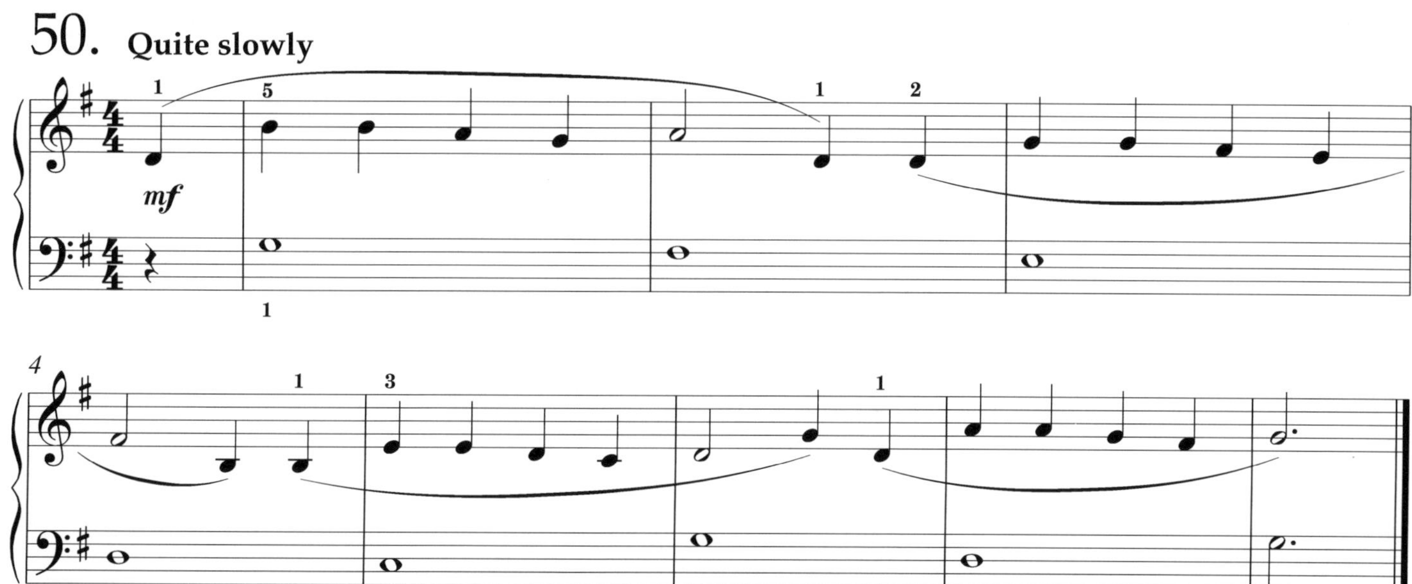

## 51. Andante

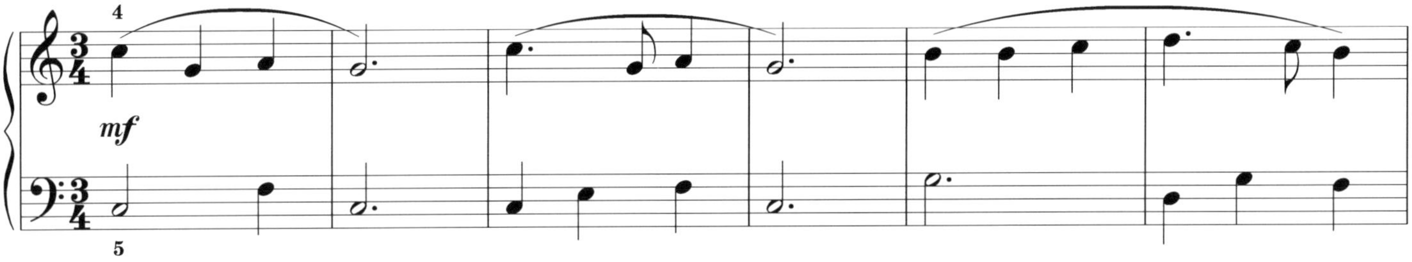

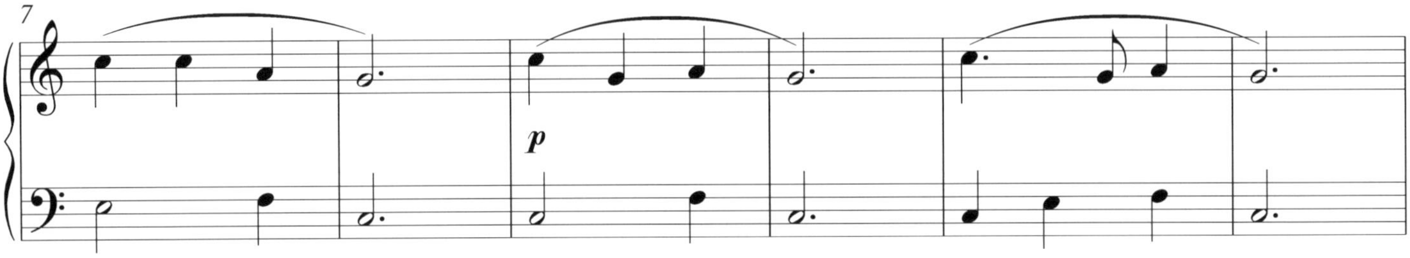

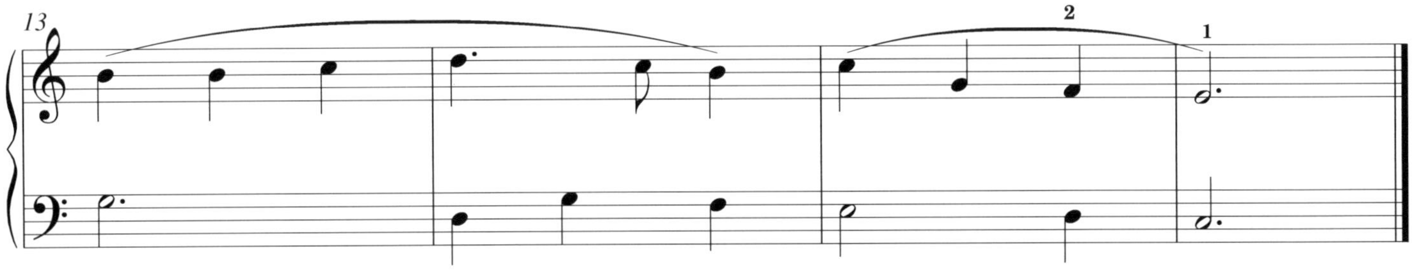

Remember, always clap, tap or sing the rhythm first.

N'oubliez pas de toujours d'abord battre, frapper dans les mains ou chanter le rythme.

Denk daran – immer zuerst den Rhythmus klatschen, klopfen oder singen.

## 52. Legato

# 5. Position changes in the left hand
# 5. Changement de position à la main gauche
# *5. Positionswechsel in der linken Hand*

**Remember:**
**Always** look at the *time signature* first.
**Always** clap, tap or sing the *rhythm.*
**Always** check the *key signature.*
Where are the *sharps* and *flats?*
**Always** be aware of the *key* you are playing in.
**Always** find the *correct position* for each hand to begin.
**Always** try to *watch the music* and not your hands!

**Rappels:**
**Toujours** regarder l'indication de *mesure* d'abord.
**Toujours** battre le *rythme* ou le frapper dans les mains ou le chanter.
**Toujours** vérifier *l'armure* de la clef, quels sont les *dièses* ou les *bémol.*
**Toujours** garder à l'esprit de *tonalité* dans laquelle on joue.
**Toujours** rechercher la *position correcte* de chaque main pour commencer.
**Toujours** s'efforcer de *lire la musique* et de ne pas regarder les mains!

**Denk daran:**
**Immer** zuerst nach der *Taktvorzeichnung* sehen.
**Immer** den *Rhythmus* klatschen, klopfen oder singen.
**Immer** die *Tonartvorzeichnung* beachten.
Wo stehen *Kreuze* und ♭*'s?*
**Immer** die *Tonart* merken, in der man spielt.
**Immer** für jede Hand die *richtige Position* herausfinden, mit der man anfängt.
**Immer** versuchen, auf die *Noten zu sehen* und nicht auf die eigene Hände!

## 56. Cantabile

## 57. With movement

58. Flowing
mp
59. Slow and solemn
mp
lightly detached
(sim.)

Try to play musically and expressively.

Essayez de jouer avec musicalité et expression.

Versuche, musikalisch und ausdrucksvoll zu spielen.

# 6. Simple position changes in both hands
# 6. Changements de position simples aux deux mains
# *6. Einfache Positionswechsel in beiden Händen*

**Remember:**
**Always** look at the *time signature* first.
**Always** clap, tap or sing the *rhythm.*
**Always** check the *key signature.*
Where are the *sharps* and *flats?*
**Always** be aware of the *key* you are playing in.
**Always** find the *correct position* for each hand to begin.
**Always** try to *watch the music* and not your hands!

**Rappels:**
**Toujours** regarder l'indication de *mesure* d'abord.
**Toujours** battre le *rythme* ou le frapper dans les mains ou le chanter.
**Toujours** vérifier *l'armure* de la clef, quels sont les *dièses* ou les *bémol.*
**Toujours** garder à l'esprit de *tonalité* dans laquelle on joue.
**Toujours** rechercher la *position correcte* de chaque main pour commencer.
**Toujours** s'efforcer de *lire la musique* et de ne pas regarder les mains!

**Denk daran:**
**Immer** zuerst nach der *Taktvorzeichnung* sehen.
**Immer** den *Rhythmus* klatschen, klopfen oder singen.
**Immer** die *Tonartvorzeichnung* beachten. Wo stehen *Kreuze* und *♭'s?*
**Immer** die *Tonart* merken, in der man spielt.
**Immer** für jede Hand die *richtige Position* herausfinden, mit der man anfängt.
**Immer** versuchen, auf die *Noten zu sehen* und nicht auf die eigene Hände!

66. Sadly
mp
p
mf
p
67. In canon
mf
mf

Set yourself a realistic tempo. Always look at the tempo/style indication given

Prenez un tempo raisonnable. Regardez toujours les indications de tempo et de style données.

Wähle ein realistisches Tempo. Achte immer auf die notierten Tempo/Stilangaben.

## 69. Adagio

*lightly detached*

*p*

*mf*

## 70. Adagio

## 71. March

## 72. Gracefully

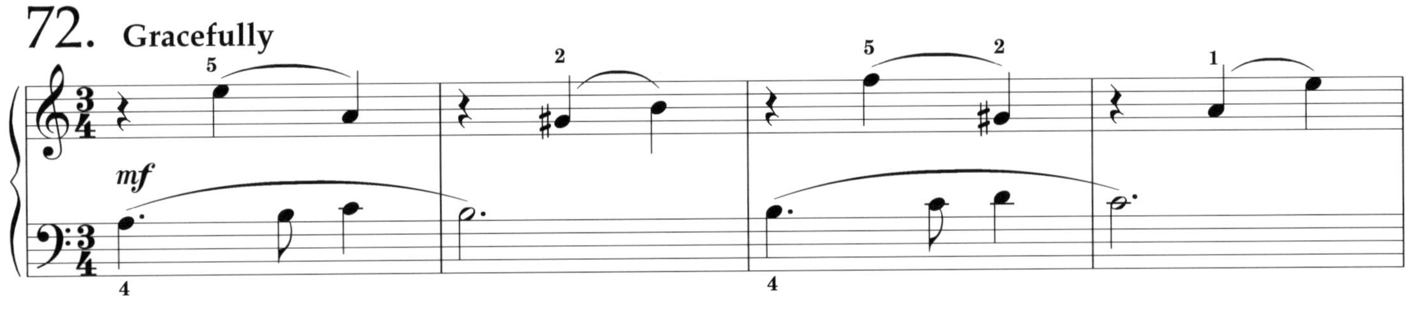

# 7. Introducing chords – 2nds and 3rds
# 7. Initiation aux accords – intervalles de secondes et de tierces
# *7. Einführung von Akkorden – Sekunden und Terzen*

**Remember:**
**Always** look at the *time signature* first.
**Always** clap, tap or sing the *rhythm.*
**Always** check the *key signature.*
Where are the *sharps* and *flats?*
**Always** be aware of the *key* you are playing in.
**Always** find the *correct position* for each hand to begin.
**Always** try to *watch the music* and not your hands!

**Rappels:**
**Toujours** regarder l'indication de *mesure* d'abord.
**Toujours** battre le *rythme* ou le frapper dans les mains ou le chanter.
**Toujours** vérifier *l'armure* de la clef, quels sont les *dièses* ou les *bémol.*
**Toujours** garder à l'esprit de *tonalité* dans laquelle on joue.
**Toujours** rechercher la *position correcte* de chaque main pour commencer.
**Toujours** s'efforcer de *lire la musique* et de ne pas regarder les mains!

**Denk daran:**
**Immer** zuerst nach der *Taktvorzeichnung* sehen.
**Immer** den *Rhythmus* klatschen, klopfen oder singen.
**Immer** die *Tonartvorzeichnung* beachten. Wo stehen *Kreuze* und ♭*'s?*
**Immer** die *Tonart* merken, in der man spielt.
**Immer** für jede Hand die *richtige Position* herausfinden, mit der man anfängt.
**Immer** versuchen, auf die *Noten zu sehen* und nicht auf die eigene Hände!

## 73. In Waltz time

## 74. Moderato

## 75. Flowing

## 76. Andante

Do you know which key you are in? The last and lowest note is usually a reliable guide.

Savez-vous dans quelle tonalité vous êtes? La dernière note la plus grave est généralement une indication fiable.

Weißt du, in welcher Tonart du dich befindest? Die letzte und niedrigste Note ist in der Regel ein guter Anhaltspunkt.

## 77. Flowing

## 78. Dolce

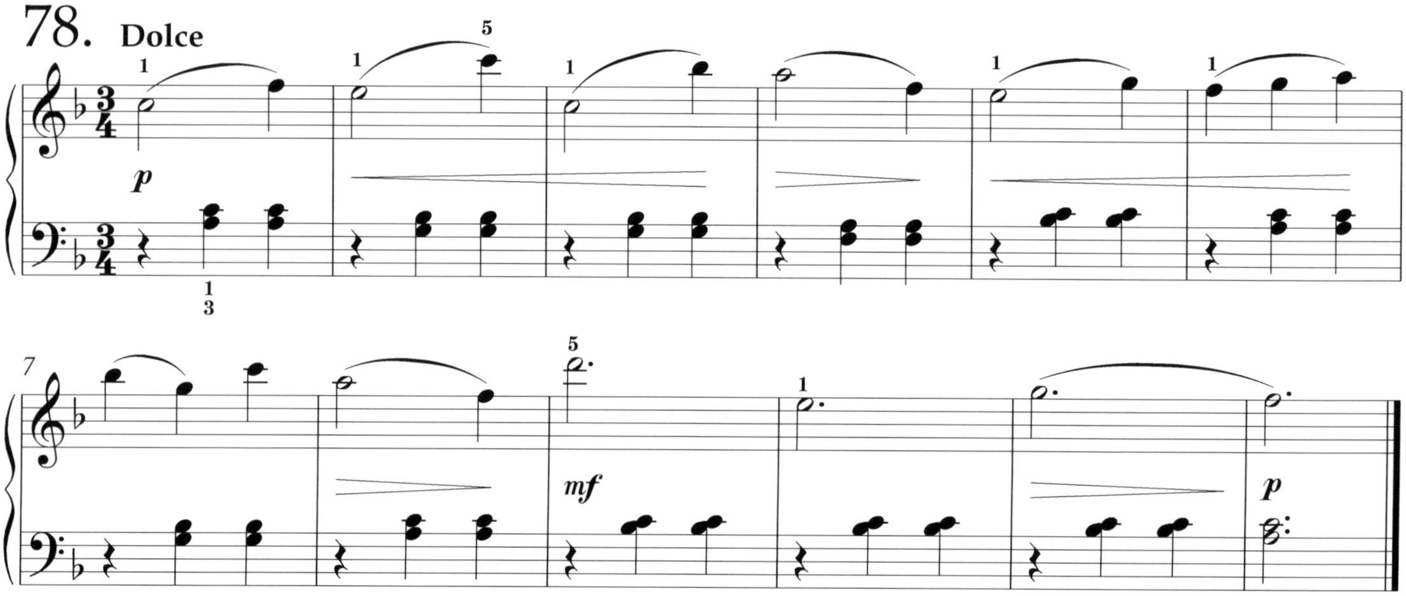

## 79. Cantabile

*lightly detached*

Try to play musically and expressively.

Essayez de jouer avec musicalité et expression.

Versuche, musikalisch und ausdrucksvoll zu spielen.

## 80. Maestoso

# 8. Introducing chords – 4ths and 6ths
# 8. Initiation aux accords – intervalles de quartes et de sixtes
# *8. Einführung von Akkorden – Quarten und Sexten*

**Remember:**
**Always** look at the *time signature* first.
**Always** clap, tap or sing the *rhythm.*
**Always** check the *key signature.*
Where are the *sharps* and *flats?*
**Always** be aware of the *key* you are playing in.
**Always** find the *correct position* for each hand to begin.
**Always** try to *watch the music* and not your hands!

**Rappels:**
**Toujours** regarder l'indication de *mesure* d'abord.
**Toujours** battre le *rythme* ou le frapper dans les mains ou le chanter.
**Toujours** vérifier *l'armure* de la clef, quels sont les *dièses* ou les *bémol.*
**Toujours** garder à l'esprit de *tonalité* dans laquelle on joue.
**Toujours** rechercher la *position correcte* de chaque main pour commencer.
**Toujours** s'efforcer de *lire la musique* et de ne pas regarder les mains!

**Denk daran:**
**Immer** zuerst nach der *Taktvorzeichnung* sehen.
**Immer** den *Rhythmus* klatschen, klopfen oder singen.
**Immer** die *Tonartvorzeichnung* beachten. Wo stehen *Kreuze* und ♭'s?
**Immer** die *Tonart* merken, in der man spielt.
**Immer** für jede Hand die *richtige Position* herausfinden, mit der man anfängt.
**Immer** versuchen, auf die *Noten zu sehen* und nicht auf die eigene Hände!

84. Flowing
mp
con Ped.
85. Smoothly
p
con Ped.
pp

86. Simply
p
87. With a slow blues feel
p
88. Leisurely
p

89. Unhurried
p
90. Relaxed – with swing quavers
mp
con Ped.

91. Leisurely
p legato
mf
p
92. Poco lento
mf
93. Expressively
mp

94. Dreamily
p
mf
p
rall.
95. Largo
p
con Pedale
mf
p

# 9. Introducing chords – 5ths and 7ths

# 9. Initiation aux accords – intervalles de quintes et de septièmes

# *9. Einführung von Akkorden – Quinten und Septen*

**Remember:**
**Always** look at the *time signature* first.
**Always** clap, tap or sing the *rhythm.*
**Always** check the *key signature.* Where are the *sharps* and *flats?*
**Always** be aware of the *key* you are playing in.
**Always** find the *correct position* for each hand to begin.
**Always** try to *watch the music* and not your hands!

**Rappels:**
**Toujours** regarder l'indication de *mesure* d'abord.
**Toujours** battre le *rythme* ou le frapper dans les mains ou le chanter.
**Toujours** vérifier *l'armure* de la clef, quels sont les *dièses* ou les *bémol.*
**Toujours** garder à l'esprit de *tonalité* dans laquelle on joue.
**Toujours** rechercher la *position correcte* de chaque main pour commencer.
**Toujours** s'efforcer de *lire la musique* et de ne pas regarder les mains!

**Denk daran:**
**Immer** zuerst nach der *Taktvorzeichnung* sehen.
**Immer** den *Rhythmus* klatschen, klopfen oder singen.
**Immer** die *Tonartvorzeichnung* beachten. Wo stehen *Kreuze* und ♭*'s?*
**Immer** die *Tonart* merken, in der man spielt.
**Immer** für jede Hand die *richtige Position* herausfinden, mit der man anfängt.
**Immer** versuchen, auf die *Noten zu sehen* und nicht auf die eigene Hände!

9
rall.
99. Dreamily
p sempre
con Ped.
6
100. Brightly
mf
p
7
f
p
12

# 10. Introducing various 2-note chords
# 10. Introduction de divers intervalles plaqués
# *10. Einführung verschiedener Zweitonakkorde*

**Remember:**
**Always** look at the *time signature* first.
**Always** clap, tap or sing the *rhythm.*
**Always** check the *key signature.*
Where are the *sharps* and *flats?*
**Always** be aware of the *key* you are playing in.
**Always** find the *correct position* for each hand to begin.
**Always** try to *watch the music* and not your hands!

**Rappels:**
**Toujours** regarder l'indication de *mesure* d'abord.
**Toujours** battre le *rythme* ou le frapper dans les mains ou le chanter.
**Toujours** vérifier *l'armure* de la clef, quels sont les *dièses* ou les *bémol.*
**Toujours** garder à l'esprit de *tonalité* dans laquelle on joue.
**Toujours** rechercher la *position correcte* de chaque main pour commencer.
**Toujours** s'efforcer de *lire la musique* et de ne pas regarder les mains!

**Denk daran:**
**Immer** zuerst nach der *Taktvorzeichnung* sehen.
**Immer** den *Rhythmus* klatschen, klopfen oder singen.
**Immer** die *Tonartvorzeichnung* beachten. Wo stehen *Kreuze* und *♭'s?*
**Immer** die *Tonart* merken, in der man spielt.
**Immer** für jede Hand die *richtige Position* herausfinden, mit der man anfängt.
**Immer** versuchen, auf die *Noten zu sehen* und nicht auf die eigene Hände!

104. Not too fast
p
mf cantabile
105. Allegretto
mp
f
mf
p
106. Adagio
p legato
p

# 11. Introducing triads and inversions
# 11. Initiation aux accords de trois sons et aux renversements
# *11. Einführung von Dreiklängen und Umkehrungen*

3-note chords and their fingering

Les accords de trois sons et leur doigtés

Dreitonakkorde mit Fingersatz

C major / Do majeur / C-Dur

5 3 1 or / ou / oder 4 2 1

| root position<br>Etat fondamental<br>Grundstellung | 1st inversion<br>Premier renvers.<br>1. Umkehrung | 2nd inversion<br>Deuxième renvers.<br>2. Umkehrung |
|---|---|---|

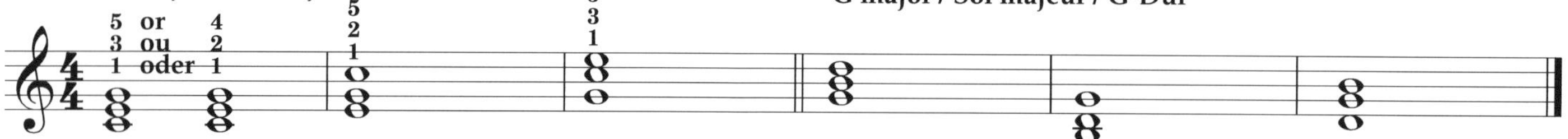

G major / Sol majeur / G-Dur

| root pos.<br>Etat fondamental<br>Grundstellung | 1st inv.<br>Premier renvers.<br>1. Umkehrung | 2nd inv.<br>Deuxième renvers.<br>2. Umkehrung |
|---|---|---|

F major / Fa majeur / F-Dur

| root pos.<br>Etat fondamental<br>Grundstellung | 1st inv.<br>Premier renvers.<br>1. Umkehrung | 2nd inv.<br>Deuxième renvers.<br>2. Umkehrung |
|---|---|---|

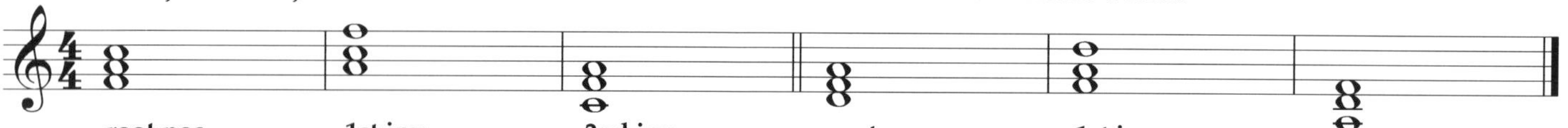

D minor / Re mineur / d-Moll

| root pos.<br>Etat fondamental<br>Grundstellung | 1st inv.<br>Premier renvers.<br>1. Umkehrung | 2nd inv.<br>Deuxième renvers.<br>2. Umkehrung |
|---|---|---|

E minor / Mi mineur / e-Moll

| root pos.<br>Etat fondamental<br>Grundstellung | 1st inv.<br>Premier renvers.<br>1. Umkehrung | 2nd inv.<br>Deuxième renvers.<br>2. Umkehrung |
|---|---|---|

Other chords used / Autres accords employés / Sonstige Akkorde

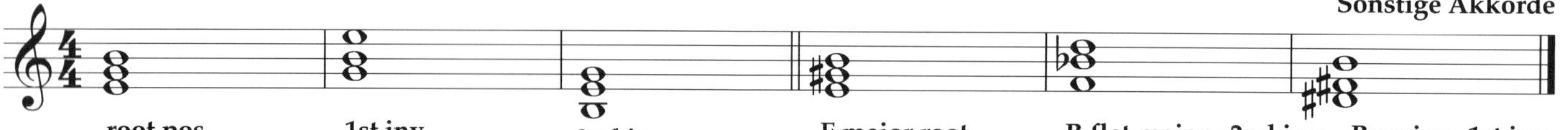

| E major root<br>Mi-maj. état fond.<br>E-Dur-Grund-stellung | B flat major - 2nd inv.<br>si bémol majeur<br>B-Dur-<br>2. Umkehrung | B major - 1st inv.<br>si majeur premier renv.<br>H-Dur-<br>1. Umkehrung |
|---|---|---|

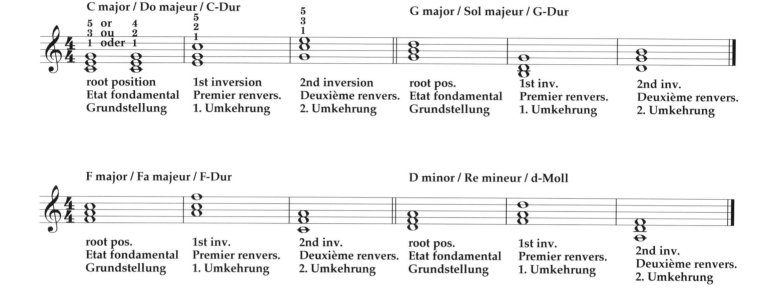

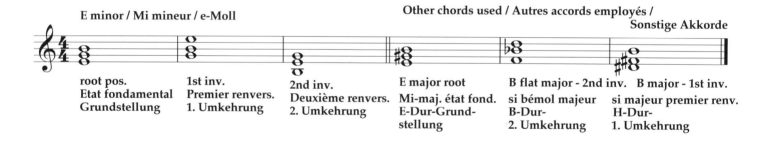

## Fingering for left-hand triads
## Doigtés des accords de trois sons à la main gauche
## Fingersatz für Dreiklänge in der linken Hand

C major · Do majeur · C-Dur

1 3 5 or / ou / oder 1 2 4

| root pos.<br>Etat fondamental<br>Grundstellung | 1st inv.<br>Premier renvers.<br>1. Umkehrung | 2nd inv.<br>Deuxième renvers.<br>2. Umkehrung |
|---|---|---|

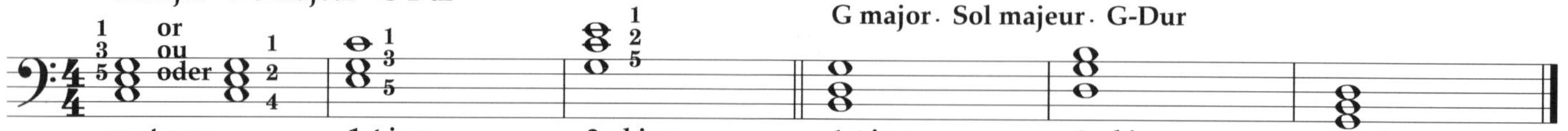

G major · Sol majeur · G-Dur

| 1st inv.<br>Premier renvers.<br>1. Umkehrung | 2nd inv.<br>Deuxième renvers.<br>2. Umkehrung | root pos.<br>Etat fondamental<br>Grundstellung |
|---|---|---|

## 107. In March style

108. Maestoso
f
4
2
1
1
109. Majestically
mf
5
2
110. Dolce
p
6
12
111. In Waltz time
p
mf
4
4
2

# 12. Introducing dominant 7th chords
# 12. Initiation aux accords de septième de dominante
# *12. Einführung von Dominantseptakkorden*

**Remember:**
**Always** look at the *time signature* first.
**Always** clap, tap or sing the *rhythm.*
**Always** check the *key signature.* Where are the *sharps* and *flats?*
**Always** be aware of the *key* you are playing in.
**Always** find the *correct position* for each hand to begin.
**Always** try to *watch the music* and not your hands!

**Rappels:**
**Toujours** regarder l'indication de *mesure* d'abord.
**Toujours** battre le *rythme* ou le frapper dans les mains ou le chanter.
**Toujours** vérifier *l'armure* de la clef, quels sont les *dièses* ou les *bémol.*
**Toujours** garder à l'esprit de *tonalité* dans laquelle on joue.
**Toujours** rechercher la *position correcte* de chaque main pour commencer.
**Toujours** s'efforcer de *lire la musique* et de ne pas regarder les mains!

**Denk daran:**
**Immer** zuerst nach der *Taktvorzeichnung* sehen.
**Immer** den *Rhythmus* klatschen, klopfen oder singen.
**Immer** die *Tonartvorzeichnung* beachten. Wo stehen *Kreuze* und ♭'s?
**Immer** die *Tonart* merken, in der man spielt.
**Immer** für jede Hand die *richtige Position* herausfinden, mit der man anfängt.
**Immer** versuchen, auf die *Noten zu sehen* und nicht auf die eigene Hände!

## 112. Gracefully

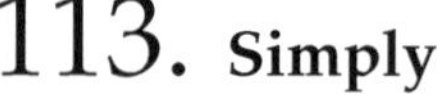

## 113. Simply

114. Slowly
3
mp
1
9
p
5
5
115. Not too fast
3
1
5
mf
1
5
116. Simply
3
3
9
3

# 13. The key of E minor
# 13. La tonalité de mi mineur
# *13. Die Tonart e-Moll*

**Remember:**
**Always** look at the *time signature* first.
**Always** clap, tap or sing the *rhythm.*
**Always** check the *key signature.*
Where are the *sharps* and *flats?*
**Always** be aware of the *key* you are playing in.
**Always** find the *correct position* for each hand to begin.
**Always** try to *watch the music* and not your hands!

**Rappels:**
**Toujours** regarder l'indication de *mesure* d'abord.
**Toujours** battre le *rythme* ou le frapper dans les mains ou le chanter.
**Toujours** vérifier *l'armure* de la clef, quels sont les *dièses* ou les *bémol.*
**Toujours** garder à l'esprit de *tonalité* dans laquelle on joue.
**Toujours** rechercher la *position correcte* de chaque main pour commencer.
**Toujours** s'efforcer de *lire la musique* et de ne pas regarder les mains!

**Denk daran:**
**Immer** zuerst nach der *Taktvorzeichnung* sehen.
**Immer** den *Rhythmus* klatschen, klopfen oder singen.
**Immer** die *Tonartvorzeichnung* beachten. Wo stehen *Kreuze* und *♭'s?*
**Immer** die *Tonart* merken, in der man spielt.
**Immer** für jede Hand die *richtige Position* herausfinden, mit der man anfängt.
**Immer** versuchen, auf die *Noten zu sehen* und nicht auf die eigene Hände!

120. Lively
mf
f
121. Con brio
f
122. Allegretto
mf
p
mf
p

# 14. The key of B minor
# 14. Le tonalité de si mineur
# *14. Die Tonart h-Moll*

**Remember:**
**Always** look at the *time signature* first.
**Always** clap, tap or sing the *rhythm.*
**Always** check the *key signature.*
Where are the *sharps* and *flats?*
**Always** be aware of the *key* you are playing in.
**Always** find the *correct position* for each hand to begin.
**Always** try to *watch the music* and not your hands!

**Rappels:**
**Toujours** regarder l'indication de *mesure* d'abord.
**Toujours** battre le *rythme* ou le frapper dans les mains ou le chanter.
**Toujours** vérifier *l'armure* de la clef, quels sont les *dièses* ou les *bémol.*
**Toujours** garder à l'esprit de *tonalité* dans laquelle on joue.
**Toujours** rechercher la *position correcte* de chaque main pour commencer.
**Toujours** s'efforcer de *lire la musique* et de ne pas regarder les mains!

**Denk daran:**
**Immer** zuerst nach der *Taktvorzeichnung* sehen.
**Immer** den *Rhythmus* klatschen, klopfen oder singen.
**Immer** die *Tonartvorzeichnung* beachten. Wo stehen *Kreuze* und *♭'s?*
**Immer** die *Tonart* merken, in der man spielt.
**Immer** für jede Hand die *richtige Position* herausfinden, mit der man anfängt.
**Immer** versuchen, auf die *Noten zu sehen* und nicht auf die eigene Hände!

7
12
Remember, always clap, tap or sing the rhythm first.
N'oubliez pas de toujours d'abord battre, frapper dans les mains ou chanter le rythme.
Denk daran – immer zuerst den Rhythmus klatschen, klopfen oder singen.
126. In March time
f
5
127. Slow and sustained
mp
con Ped.
5

## 128. Moderato

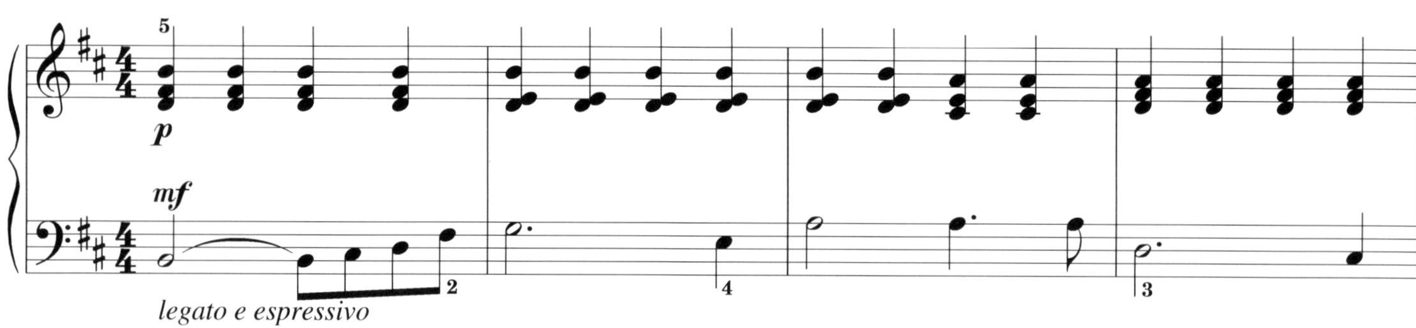

It will always help to count a full bar before you begin.

Il sera toujours utile de compter une mesure complète avant de commencer.

Es hilft immer, einen ganzen Takt zu zählen, bevor man zu spielen anfängt.

## 129. With expression

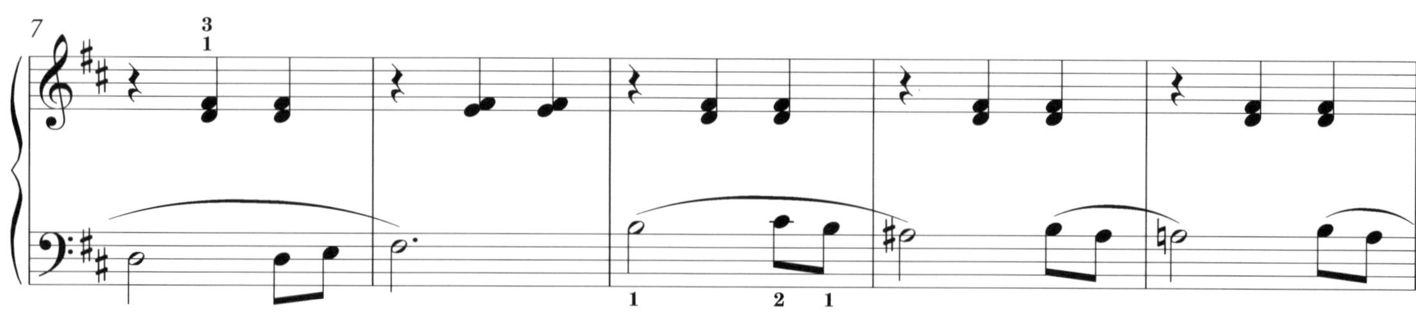

130. Vivace
mf
131. Gavotte
f
p
f
p
f
132. Solemnly
p legato
con Ped.

# 15. The key of B flat major
# 15. Le tonalité de si bémol majeur
# *15. Die Tonart B-Dur*

**Remember:**
**Always** look at the *time signature* first.
**Always** clap, tap or sing the *rhythm.*
**Always** check the *key signature.*
Where are the *sharps* and *flats?*
**Always** be aware of the *key* you are playing in.
**Always** find the *correct position* for each hand to begin.
**Always** try to *watch the music* and not your hands!

**Rappels:**
**Toujours** regarder l'indication de *mesure* d'abord.
**Toujours** battre le *rythme* ou le frapper dans les mains ou le chanter.
**Toujours** vérifier *l'armure* de la clef, quels sont les *dièses* ou les *bémol.*
**Toujours** garder à l'esprit de *tonalité* dans laquelle on joue.
**Toujours** rechercher la *position correcte* de chaque main pour commencer.
**Toujours** s'efforcer de *lire la musique* et de ne pas regarder les mains!

**Denk daran:**
**Immer** zuerst nach der *Taktvorzeichnung* sehen.
**Immer** den *Rhythmus* klatschen, klopfen oder singen.
**Immer** die *Tonartvorzeichnung* beachten. Wo stehen *Kreuze* und ♭'s?
**Immer** die *Tonart* merken, in der man spielt.
**Immer** für jede Hand die *richtige Position* herausfinden, mit der man anfängt.
**Immer** versuchen, auf die *Noten zu sehen* und nicht auf die eigene Hände!

## 133. Brightly

## 134. Flowing

## 135. Lively

136. In Waltz time
mf
p
mf
137. Allegretto
mf
p
f
138. Gavotte
mf
f
p

139. Expressively
p
mf legato
140. Flowing
mp
p
p
mf
141. Giocoso

## 142. With movement

## 143. Flowing

## 144. Vivace

## 16. The key of G minor
## 16. Le tonalité de sol mineur
## *16. Die Tonart g-Moll*

**Remember:**
**Always** look at the *time signature* first.
**Always** clap, tap or sing the *rhythm.*
**Always** check the *key signature.*
Where are the *sharps* and *flats?*
**Always** be aware of the *key* you are playing in.
**Always** find the *correct position* for each hand to begin.
**Always** try to *watch the music* and not your hands!

**Rappels:**
**Toujours** regarder l'indication de *mesure* d'abord.
**Toujours** battre le *rythme* ou le frapper dans les mains ou le chanter.
**Toujours** vérifier *l'armure* de la clef, quels sont les *dièses* ou les *bémol.*
**Toujours** garder à l'esprit de *tonalité* dans laquelle on joue.
**Toujours** rechercher la *position correcte* de chaque main pour commencer.
**Toujours** s'efforcer de *lire la musique* et de ne pas regarder les mains!

**Denk daran:**
**Immer** zuerst nach der *Taktvorzeichnung* sehen.
**Immer** den *Rhythmus* klatschen, klopfen oder singen.
**Immer** die *Tonartvorzeichnung* beachten.
Wo stehen *Kreuze* und *♭'s?*
**Immer** die *Tonart* merken, in der man spielt.
**Immer** für jede Hand die *richtige Position* herausfinden, mit der man anfängt.
**Immer** versuchen, auf die *Noten zu sehen* und nicht auf die eigene Hände!

## 145. Mesto

It will always help to count a full bar before you begin.

Il sera toujours utile de compter une mesure complète avant de commencer.

Es hilft immer, einen ganzen Takt zu zählen, bevor man zu spielen anfängt.

## 146. Adagio

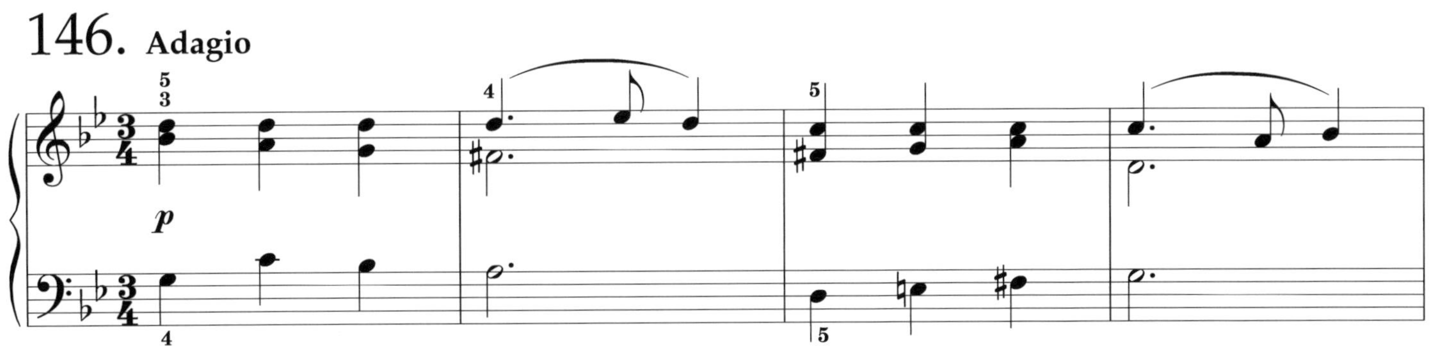

## 147. Moderato

## 148. Lively

Set yourself a realistic tempo. Always look at the tempo/style indication given

Prenez un tempo raisonnable. Regardez toujours les indications de tempo et de style données.

Wähle ein realistisches Tempo. Achte immer auf die notierten Tempo/Stilangaben.

## 149. With a lilt

Try to play musically and expressively.

Essayez de jouer avec musicalité et expression.

Versuche, musikalisch und ausdrucksvoll zu spielen.

## 150. With movement